MW00774628

73

The Madness Vase
a collection of poetry

ℭ

by Andrea Gibson

Write Bloody Publishing
America's Independent Press

Long Beach, CA

WRITEBLOODY.COM

Gibson, Andrea.
2nd edition.
ISBN: 978-1-935904-37-3

Interior Layout by Lea C. Deschenes
Cover Designed by Amy Thompson
Proofread by Lisa Losorelli and Jennifer Roach
Type set in Bergamo from www.theleagueofmoveabletype.com

Special thanks to Lightning Bolt Donor, Weston Renoud

Write Bloody Publishing
Long Beach, CA
Support Independent Presses
writebloody.com

To contact the author, send an email to writebloody@gmail.com

for Em, thank you

The Madness Vase

THE MADNESS VASE

"I'm thinking of the night that all the lights went out and how I learned to see in the dark."

—Chris Pureka

The Madness Vase

The nutritionist said I should eat root vegetables.
Said if I could get down thirteen turnips a day
I would be grounded, rooted.
Said my head would not keep flying away
to where the darkness lives.

The psychic told me my heart carries too much weight.
Said for twenty dollars she'd tell me what to do.
I handed her the twenty. She said, "Stop worrying, darling.
You will find a good man soon."

The first psycho therapist told me to spend
three hours each day sitting in a dark closet
with my eyes closed and my ears plugged.
I tried it once but couldn't stop thinking
about how gay it was to be sitting in the closet.

The yogi told me to stretch everything but the truth.
Said to focus on the out breath. Said everyone finds happiness
when they care more about what they give
than what they get.

The pharmacist said, "Lexapro, Lamictal, Lithium, Xanax."

The doctor said an anti-psychotic might help me
forget what the trauma said.

The trauma said, "Don't write these poems.
Nobody wants to hear you cry
about the grief inside your bones."

But my bones said, "Tyler Clementi jumped
from the George Washington Bridge
into the Hudson River convinced
he was entirely alone."

My bones said, "Write the poems."

THANK GOODNESS
Inspired by and written for Buddy Wakefield

At the end of your ten-day meditation retreat
you got in your car
drove thirty peaceful feet
and ran over a bird,

splayed its holy guts on the pavement
like god was finger-painting *"Fuck you"*
across that deep breath
you were holding
the way your mother held her first born.

You

thank goodness,
were torn from the Bible
the day before they burned it
for the verse about dancing to tambourines.

Once you saw the blood of Christ
on a knife carving redwood trees into church pews.
Now every Sunday morning
you hear glaciers melting
and you cry easier than a one-night stand
never, ever is
when you see the feathers in your rear view mirror
scattering like prayers
searching for a safe place to land.

Hold me to my word
when I tell you I will leave today,
catch a bus ticket west
just to stand in the center of your highway
stopping traffic 'til every feather's answered.

I've seen too many prayers
caught in the grills of eighteen-wheelers.
Folks like us, we may have
shoulder blades that rust in the rain
but they're still G-sharp
whenever our spinal chords are tuned
to the key of redemption.

So go ahead, world, pick us
to make things better.

We've been building a bridge
through the center of this song
since Mother Theresa replaced the walls of her church
with the orphaned cries of weeping ghettos.

You wanna know what the right wing never got?
We never question the existence of god.

What we question is his bulldozer
turning Palestine into a gas chamber.
What we question is the manger in Macy's
and the sweatshops our children call the North Pole.

What we question are the sixty swollen lashes
on the back of a girl found guilty of the crime
of *allowing* herself to be brutally raped.

What we question is the idea of a heaven
having gates.

Silly.

Have you never stood on the end of pier
watching the moon live up to her name?
Have you never looked in the eyes of a thief
and seen his children's hungry bellies?

Some days my heart beats so fast
my ribcage sounds like a fucking railroad track
and my breath is a train I just can't catch.

So when my friends go filling their lungs with yes,
when they're peeling off their armor
and falling like snowflakes on your holy tongue, god,
collect the feathers.

We are thick skin
covering nothing but wishbones.
Break in. You'll find
notebooks full of jaw lines
we wrote to religion's clenched fist.

Yeah, we bruise easy.
But the sound of our bouncing back
is a Grand Canyon full of choir claps
and our five-pointed stars
have always been open to the answer,
whatever it is.

I know David argued with the chisel.
I know he said, "Make me softer.
When those tourists come looking for a hero
I want the rain to puddle in my pores."

Build me holy like that.
Build me a kite flown out a bedroom window at midnight
the day freedom set its curfew to 9:11.

My heaven is a snow globe.
The blizzard will always be worth the touch of a hand
shaking me awake
like a boy taking deep breaths
all the way down to the dents in his shins
like he's building a telephone
from a string and two tin cans.

He knows god's number by heart.
He knows it isn't listed in any book.

Look me in the bull's-eye,
in the laws I broke
and the promises I didn't,
in the batteries I found when the lights went out
and the prayers I found when the brakes did, too.

I've got this moment
and no idea when it will end,
but every second of this life
is scripture.

And to know that, trust me,
we don't need to be born
again.

CRAB APPLE PIRATES

We were chubby faced school kids,
Snicker bar windpiped, crab apple pirates,
backward baseball capped, knee-scraped snow angels,
Dukes of Hazard dreamers,
bumper car bodied salamander catchers,
Michael Jordan believers.

I couldn't fly, but my hang time was three minutes
and ten seconds.

Smart kids were stupid.
Books were trees cut down.
I was a tomboy in love with Malcolm Cushion.
He had a birthmark in the shape of Canada on his left cheek.
The teachers didn't trust him.
His mother was the accidental broken tooth in a bar fight.

I had one black friend.
Her name was Erica.
She had a jackknife.
She carved a gash into the center of her palm,
another into mine, pressed our hands together
and asked if I thought it would turn her blood white.
I couldn't read her fear, or hope.
I thought history was over.
I cried during *The National Anthem.*

Once I found a butterfly's wing on the sidewalk.
I wanted to keep it but I didn't.
I knew there were things I should never find beautiful.
Like death. And girls.

On Saturdays I walked around town with a wheelbarrow
collecting aluminum cans.
On Sundays my father paid a penny for every cigarette butt
I'd pick up on the driveway.
I was picking up cigarette butts

when Tommy Chambers punched my tooth out.
I spit on his bike seat and beat the crap out of his older brother.

I started writing songs,
recorded them on my "ghetto blaster"
and mailed the tapes to the local radio station,
but they never played them
because they never had good taste.

My mother did.
She was a secretary.
Her fingernails were red
and she loved my father,
who became a mailman after the war.
When I was a baby my mother
would carry me to the post office
and weigh me on the postal scales.

Once, years later, I got lost in the mail.
The next day I came home from college
and corrected my father's grammar.

When I was ten my mother had another daughter.
I had heard babies sometimes die in their sleep
so at night when my parents went to bed
I'd put on my Karate Kid kimono
and sneak into her room to guard her heartbeat.

The heartbeat thieves didn't find her
for fifteen years.

At eleven I discovered beer.
At fourteen I accepted Jesus Christ as my personal Lord and Savior.
At nineteen I nailed my palm to Amanda Bucker's vagina,
actually drooled on her breast,
and said yes so loud god couldn't disagree.

But my family did.
So I lost them for a while, and in that while
my uncle Barry lost his fingers to the paper mill.
My uncle Peter lost his liver to Vietnam.
My mother lost her legs to god's will.

In her will I inherit everything:
the seventeen photographs we didn't lose in the fire,
all of them with charcoaled edges.
My mother holds them to her chest and tells
me she can still smell the smoke.

I tell her I will guard them well,
my father's freckled shoulders,
my sister's brown, brown eyes,
my mother's patient hands
buckling my tiny, blue suspenders,

that one December when we built a bonfire
in the middle of the frozen lake
and I skated around the flames
with my snowsuit's frozen zipper sticking to
my tongue.

My mother said, "Smile for the camera."
I can still remember the flash.
And that enormous fire
with the ice beneath it
that didn't even crack.

Maybe I Need You

The winter I told you I think icicles are magic
you stole an enormous one from a neighbors drooping shingle
and gave it to me as a gift.

I kept it in my freezer for seven months
'til the day I hurt my leg
and needed something to reduce the swelling.

Love
isn't always magic.
Sometimes it's just melting.
Where it's black and blue.
Where it hurts the most.

Last night I saw your ghost
peddling a bicycle with a basket
towards a moon as full as my heavy head
and I wanted nothing more
than to be sitting in that basket
like ET, with my glowing heart glowing right through
my chest, and my glowing finger
pointing in the direction
of our home.

Two years ago I said, "I never want
to write our break-up poem."
You built me a time capsule full of Big League Chew
and promised to never burst my bubble.

I loved you from our first date
at the batting cages
when I missed twenty-three balls in a row
and you looked at me like I was a home run
in the ninth inning of the World Series.

Now every time I hear the word love
I think, *going, going…*

The first week you were gone
I kept seeing your hand wave goodbye
like a windshield wiper in a flooding car
in the last real moment I believed
the hurricane would let me out alive.

Yesterday I carved your name into the surface
of an ice cube then held it against my chest
'til it melted into my aching pores.

Today I cried so hard the neighbors knocked on my door
and asked if I wanted to borrow some sugar.
I told them I left my sweet tooth in your belly button.

Love
isn't always magic.
But if I offered my body to the magician,
if I told him to cut me in half
so after that I could come to you whole
and ask for you back
would you listen
for this dark alley love song?
For the winter we heated our home
from the steam off our own bodies?

I wrote you too many poems in a language
I did not yet know how to speak

but I know now
it doesn't matter how well I say grace
if I am sitting at a table where I have no bread to eat.

So this is my wheat field.
You can have every acre, love.
This is my garden song.
This is my thunderstorm,
this is my fistfight with that bitter frost.

Tonight I begged another stage light
to become that back-alley street lamp we danced beneath
the night your warm mouth fell on my timid cheek
as I sang, "Maybe I Need You"
off key

but in tune.

Maybe I need you the way that big moon
needs that open sea.
Maybe I didn't even know I was here
'til I saw you holding me.

Give me one room to come home to.
Give me the palm of your hand.
Every strand of my hair is a kite string
and I have been blue in the face with your sky,
crying a flood over Iowa
so your mother can wake to Venice.

Love, I smashed my glass slipper
to build a stained glass window
for every wall inside my chest.

Now my heart is a pressed flower in a tattered Bible.
It is the one verse you can trust.

So I'm putting all of my words in your collection plate.
I am setting the table with bread and grace.

My knees are bent
like the corner of a page.
I am saving your place.

SLEEPING

When the flowers were stolen
from my uncle's grave
my grandmother drove to our house
and collapsed at our door
strangled as an empty Christmas stocking
wailing for her piece of coal.

I had never seen a person
so finished with god.

Her face was a massacre of grief.
Her cries like shoveled granite
chewed her shrilling throat.
"All that they left was the flag," she kept screaming.
I thought her lungs would start bleeding.

It scraped my chest clean.
Hollowed me for weeks.
Our house was the echo of a mother clawing
the floorboards for her dead son,
a downed forest in her nail beds.

At night I obsessed
on how long flowers
might survive in the hands of thieves,
spent a month in our basement
scouring for answers
in the photographs of my father in Vietnam.

He was thin as a blade,
his eyes unfiltered as the cancer
they were given for free.

Anyone could see by the freckles in his shame
that war was no place for a soldier.

The heart is no place for the talons of secrets
you can only keep in the same chamber
you keep loaded to keep your hands
from shaking the ghosts of dead children awake.

My uncle wasn't killed by bullet.
He drank himself to sleep
trying to drown out the tiny screams.
My grandmother followed him to the grave
like every mother does.

I keep thinking of them today
as I sit in my parents' living room.
My father has been home from the hospital for a week
and I was just told he slept for three years
in a field of Agent Orange
but is refusing to accept
his 10 percent veterans medical discount
because a patriot knows the cost of war,
pays for it himself.

I have written this poem before.
But always through a window,
never through an open door.

I find my mother by the stove
stirring spaghetti sauce from a jar.
I have never heard her breathing pull this hard.

Earlier in the car
when my father broke down
she turned the radio-dial up
to save him the embarrassment of his whimper.
The radio was playing "I Wanna Sex You Up."
We listened to it for three minutes at full volume.
It was hilarious

how none of us heard a word.

I don't hear many words anymore.
The president announces the end of a war
and I just stare at my mother's eyes
as my father's face
falls into the trembling trench of hands
like a boy fresh out of boot camp
who's just dropped his gun
into somebody's cradle.

When a war ends, what does that look like exactly?
Do the cells in the body stop detonating themselves?
Does the orphanage stop screaming for its mother?
When the sand in the desert has been melted down to glass
and our reflection is not something we can stand to look at
does the white flag make for a perfect blindfold?

Yesterday I was told a story
about a little girl in Iraq, six-years-old,
who cannot fall asleep
because when she does
she dreams of nothing
but the day she watched her dog
eat her neighbor's corpse.

If you told her the war is over
do you think she'd sleep?

She's seen teeth chew through a ribcage
and swallow a beating heart.
And I can buy dog tags at the mall.
I can buy camouflage at The Gap.

I can stare at the Vietnam Wall and forget
it is missing the two million names
of the two million Vietnamese slain
so I can certainly forget that little girl,
her neighbor, her dog
and whatever soldiers we choke-chained
in the opposite direction of god.

At 4 a.m. I find my father in the living room,
television blinking.
The newscaster says the number of US troops
who were killed this month at war
was outdone by the number who came home
and committed suicide.

Outside there is a flag
hanging from the front door.
My father picked it out as carefully
as he picked out my name
when he built this house.

I want to tell him I still build my spine
from the clothesline that holds his work shirts,
but I know I'd start crying.

I am exactly like him.
We both have wrinkles around our eyes
a hundred years older than our age.
We both carry ourselves like an ambulance
with someone dead inside,
always thinking we're gonna get there in time.

I didn't get here in time.
This house echoes like an empty canteen.
Flowers do not survive long in the hands of thieves.
Everything is wilting.

I look back out the window.
My father's flag is aglow in the moonlight.
I remember something I was told many years ago.
I was told that in World War II
80 percent of US soldiers
could not bring themselves
to kill an enemy soldier
they found sleeping.

Sleeping.

I want to ask my father
if he thinks that's true.

But I know he won't sleep if I do.
And he needs to sleep.

God knows, we all do.

GRAVITY

We wear our traumas
the way the guillotine
wears gravity.

Our lovers' necks
are so soft.

GLIDER PLANE
With thanks to Anis Mojgani

If you see her
tell her it doesn't snow in Colorado.
Tell her all that stuff falling from the sky
is just sawdust
from the stilts I've been carving
for my short temper.

Tell her there's a tambourine in my chest
and yes, she still shakes me.
Too bad love is an Etch A Sketch.
Good thing love is an Etch A Sketch.

If you see her tell her
I've been running towards my life
like Laura Ingalls running down that hill
in her flowered dress.

I wore a flowered dress to my birthday boy party.
Don't me look at me like that.
I'm not the box the gift came in.
This heart is my Sunday best,
grass stained from the day I discovered her neck
tasted like the reed of my first saxophone.

If I could still play, I'd play the softest song…
a moth in the lamplight,
a snow globe turning upside down,
Michelle Obama buttoning her husband's
bulletproof vest.

We are all fragile and fraying,
praying we can hold the tire swing
through the summer.
My mood swings with its feet
dangling in the river.

If you see her
tell her the moon is all her fault.
Love…a trapdoor of light,
even when it's gone, it's somewhere.

Tonight I buried her time capsule in the ball field
for every time running for home
meant running towards her.
Next time I promise I will listen
when the umpire tells me I'm safe.

Next time I will know it is normal
to have a hard time breathing
when you shake the dust.

We make everything so complicated.
Sometimes the message in the bottle
is, "Don't drink so much."
There's too much Novocaine
in our wisdom teeth already.
Every window begs to be open
when the storm comes.

I dig seed holes in my pillow
and dream this upside-down umbrella
is a teacup for god.
The puddles in my eyes
are monuments of grief
crumbling beneath moss.

You can spend your whole life
wearing a life vest in the desert.
It took me so long to burn those fire escapes.

But I know neither of us
were only the felonies on our records.
I know the music we were trying to make.
Every one of us is a Mack Truck
with a soft bed inside.

I've got my thumb out on the highway,
and I know she never drives this way.

If you see her tell her I made a song
from the dial tone.
I made a papier--mâché glider plane
from our unfinished poem.

Take the elevator to the parking garage rooftop.
Take a cigar box full of crayons
and write what you see:
the bassinet of my mouth unfurling its ribbons
to raise my voice honest. Honestly,
she was an anthem.
I was a stadium full of patriots
with their hands on their hearts.

Honestly my hand is still on my heart
as the fireworks announce the end of the game
and the colors in the sky
chase the birds inside.

Have you seen the nests they are building
from everything we left behind?

A Letter to Kelsey, Who Loves Jesus.

I have been thinking about snow angels.
About grace and melting and bloom.
About the bee that flew into my mouth
when I was riding my bicycle.
It stung my tongue
and I swore I tasted honey.

I have been thinking about the time
I climbed to the top of the church steeple
and pressed my palms on the church bell.
It was cold. And holy.
And when I touched it
my eyes could see forever.

I have been thinking
about my mother's music box.
Inside of that box there was a cross
my mother's father made for her
when she was a little girl.

Inside the cross was a winter
with a snowy road
that my mother's father used to walk down
carrying my mother on his shoulders
before he died and went to Heaven.

My grandfather went to Heaven.

I know this because he taught my mother
how to wiggle her ears.
I know this because my mother walks the same way
my grandfather did
and on the days my mother cannot get out of bed
her single comfort
is knowing she has his blood.

We are snow angels, Kelsey,
and somebody like Jesus
is down on his back in the cold making us,
arms waving like a kid in a bee's nest.

Sometimes on nights like this one
after a day like today
when I see you
moving grace through the cut of it all,
saying you love Jesus
but can no longer call yourself a Christian,

I sit down in my big orange chair
and make my fingers chase
this keyboard through the fog.

Kelsey, I imagine Heaven is a sad place
because I imagine it's full of people like you,
with hearts so big they can't help but be heavy.

I look up sometimes.
When I do I see them,
sad and bright as the sun on the swords we swallow,
carving our questions into flutes.

Answers have too many anchors.
Let's grow up to be chain-cutters.
Let's keep telling each other stories
'til we know what's true.

This is true.
I was fourteen-years-old
at the Baptist church in Calais, Maine
serving Thanksgiving dinner
to people who had no homes.

A man came in so hungry
he started drinking the coffee creamers.
When he'd drank about a dozen
the preacher's wife ran up and
scolded him for his "terrible manners."

I served the man dinner,
wished him a peaceful holiday,
and left the church.

But I talked to Jesus, Kelsey,
the whole way home.

PIANO

"The casket is a ladder," says the preacher.
I remember the ring you gave me,
how I smashed it into pieces trying to decide
if it was real.

What note could you have left
for your mother's favorite black dress
worn here?

For your brother outside the window
in the suit he wore to prom
smoking his heart into hatchet?

For your father refusing to take a tissue,
embarrassing the men with the nervous coughs?

For the car your cousin keeps calling a limo?
For your baby sister asking
why they are calling it a wake?

Last night I tore the feathers from my pillow
searching for the songs of the birds.

Morning came silent
as your bones,
and now your face, here
in this empty box,
resting like a piano on fire.

Is this the place
you wanted to go
the night I swallowed your cock like an opera
and your makeup melted from your cheekbones
onto the whiskey spilled dirt?

When you walked me home
the earth was still
between my teeth.
My lungs were an attic full of dust.

You kept flipping through
the photographs on my breath.
Everything inside me
was overexposed,
the glitter in my tough,
the slur in my family tree.

When I asked you to stay
my jaw was not a hinge.
There was nothing open in the question.

We all have bullets beneath our skin
we pray our lovers won't flinch at when they find.
We all have sirens in our light.

But if you think this is a eulogy
you haven't seen my nail beds.

I've already built too many wind chimes
from covered tailpipes
to lay anyone down that clean,

to write your release
with a pretty pen
to the pitch of your mother's scream.

The only word
I have to give you
is good-bye.

If the casket is a ladder,

climb.

WHEN THE LOVE OF YOUR LIFE LEAVES YOU

Bake a wedding cake.
Step on it.

Frost the living room floor
with your dancing feet.

Lock the front door.
Close the blinds.

Lick the floorboards.

Two Birds

"Love is the only war worth dying for." — Derrick Brown

When you ran for the border
I spent three months calling your name
'til I watched your feet leave our country
and I bunkered down in your cheerleader pajamas
to stare at our photograph
of the two birds.

Two birds.

Give me one stone,
or a rifle.

I'll collect the feathers from the ground
to make pens
to write poems about Obama.

Remember how we fucked
in the bathroom stall
during his inauguration
at Invesco Field?

Later in our seats
you held my hand and said,
"Look at Michelle. She is so in love."

There were so many snipers in the stands
when the fireworks startled us in the stairwell
I thought for sure we were being bombed.

For five minutes we sprinted
frantic through the tunnel.

I kept saying, "I love you, I love you, I love..."

I thought for certain I would turn to dust
in your arms.

Dear Love,

I hope your new home is beautiful.
I hope you rise to your feet
every time she sings her anthem.
I hope your hand is forever on your heart.
I hope your heart is forever safe.

Here at home
they are saying Obama is not the saint
we had hoped he would be.

I wonder if you'd notice
that Michelle is still in love.

Somewhere, a Carpenter

The old woman
cannot remember
swallowing her teeth.

She only knows
there is something
chewing at her stomach
and she no longer has what it takes
to eat.

Somewhere,
a carpenter
is finishing her casket.

When the sandpaper
pulls across the oak
it sounds like the lungs
of a sprinter.

The old woman knows
what she is running from,
so she no longer cares
where she is going.

Her light is still on at midnight.
I find her knitting a pair of mittens.
She always gets the thumbs just right.

My hands have never been cold.

When I was born
they gave me her name.
When I was young I thought
she'd spent her whole life
very, very old.

Now tonight,
in this tired room,
a single curl giggles
against her forehead.
Her mother's arms
are so close.

She is so ready.

"Andrea," she whispers. "Honey."
I sit down in the chair beside her,
run my palm against my shaved head.

She is the only one who didn't care
when I stopped being pretty.

"This world has too many sheep," she said,
hugged me, then went back to her knitting.

To think a sweater
is made entirely of knots.
My stomach could clothe a village tonight.
I am not ready.
The hungry never are.

When the news comes
I will tell my love
about the night years ago
when she fell from her bed
and waited on the floor until 8 a.m.
to call my mother.
She didn't want to wake her.

When my mother arrived
her leg was broken and bleeding
into the cold, wood floor.
The ambulance took her out on a stretcher.

Why is that story
most of what I will remember

when a week after her death
they open the chest beside her bed
and find it full of poems?

When everyone is wondering out loud
how they never knew she was a writer,
I will think only of the long night
she waited for the sun
to annihilate the dark,
how patiently she watched the clock
for a polite time to call,
her tender face pressed
against the hard, punishing floor.

I look down at the floor.
Her feet warm in slippers now,
tapping with the rhythm of the looping yarn.
"Who are you making the mittens for?" I ask.

She doesn't answer.
I don't mind.

I find my face in a frame on the cluttered wall.
I am giggling at the camera, so proud
of my missing teeth.

This life
is built almost entirely
of love

and losing,

isn't it?

TRELLIS
With thanks to J/J Hastain

There is a reason my body creaks like a closing casket
every time I fuck with the lights left on.

It is the same reason my friend sets fire to photographs of birds
and follows the smoke with pleading eyes.
We both had years when the phoenix didn't rise,
when we slept in beds of cindered feathers
and held hallow, ashen beaks the way other kids held ice cream cones.

I sucked the bones of a songbird's rotting wing
and you think your pills are gonna fix me, doctor?
You think I'm gonna chase this down with water?
The shame as loud as his next girl's nightmares?

I tied my tongue like a ribbon in my baby sister's hair,
like a bow around a gift I gave to my father and mother,
and my silence equaled every Christmas morning
where we were still happy and grateful.

But my silence was also his next girl's eyes
falling like timber where no one chose to hear,
her roots ripped up, her ground eroding
to the din of an old man's zipper.

Twenty years later I wake in damp sheets
my body trembling to the ghost of her voice
cracking like a frozen lake.
And I don't even know her name.
Never saw her face.
Only heard the rumors
that he'd moved on to the hemorrhage
of another perfect thing.

And now here, I sing through cinder,
through microphones raised like white flags in war zones,
through poems I've dug from my throat like fishing hooks.

From here I look back at my voice
lowered to half-mast.

How he must have stood there
with his dirty hand on his dirty heart
laughing like a broken levy
as his next girl woke with body bags beneath her eyes
and enough shame in her gut
to give the hurricane her own name.
If I could see her face,
if I could face the I of her storm
how would I ever tell her that I speak for a living?

Would I offer my own wounds as condolence?
Would I tell her his claws carved me animal?
Would I say, "At fourteen-years-old
I threw my bloody fists into my boyfriend's face
'til his eyes swelled shut
and his tears turned crimson and his jaw cracked
'til I was finally convinced his hands
were not every man's hands."

Would I tell her I have stood beneath street lamps
waiting for the swarming flies
to identify my body as carcass,
to swallow every cell of salt
and leave nothing behind but the trellis
of my untouched bones?

I remember the fault lines in the corners of his eyes,
the way he shook hands with my father,
the smirk on his face beneath the swollen sun.
Even his shadow looked guilty,
the concrete made crime scene by its touch.

Would I tell her this?
Would I ask if she has ever outlined her own body with chalk?
If there is yellow tape in her top dresser drawer
for those nights when her true love's touch
is an anthem to a dead country
and she finds herself with rope burns around your neck
begging the bodies of strangers
to not respect her in the morning?

In the morning I shovel my blood from the white snow,
I wipe my frantic breath from the window,
and bind my breasts
so that something will hold my breath so tight
not even the air in my lungs could be identified as woman.

Woman,
Are you a carbon copy of myself?
Is there a boy inside you painting your cells
with the charcoal of cindered feathers
so you will never again glow in the dark
the way girls do?

Woman,
if I knew your name,
if I could face your storm
and the warning, locked in my voice box,
that never came

would I tell you all of this?

And after that
would I ever find the nerve to admit
that even if I could
I would not take my silence back?

My father owned a gun.
He would have blown that man apart.
My mother owned a mother's heart.
Everything would have broken.

Everything but you.

ASHES

A couple of years ago, I was told a story about a soldier who was set on fire and burned to death because he was gay. After that, I started reading similar stories about people in the GLBTQ community who were tortured or killed by being set on fire and burned. I couldn't stop thinking about the people who had died that way and couldn't stop wondering what they might say from where they are now.

The night I was torn from the pages of their Bible
and burned alive
my ashes came down like snow
and a girl who had never seen my face
saw me falling from the sky
and lay down on her back
to make an angel in the powder of my bones.

From heaven I watched her,
though my eyes were still aflame,
and my ribs were still blue.
They didn't win, I whispered, as her arms built my wings.
They didn't win.
Look at that moon.
It is a pebble in my hand.
Tonight I could skip it across that fog-drunk sea
'til their lashes accordion in the light
and all they know of hate
is that it couldn't beat the love out of me...

that when they dropped me to the grave
I fell like a bucket into a well
and came up full
carving my lover's name
into the skin of a weeping willow
that spent had its entire life laughing at the rain.

Hold me like a lantern.
Staircase my spine.
When they bring their children to my funeral
to scream "FAGGOT" at my dust

tell them I was born into this casket
but I wouldn't pull the splinters from my heart
any more than Christ would have pulled the thorns
from His crimson head.

They can come a thousand times
with their burning matches and their gasoline,
with their hungry laws
and their empty mouths full of prayers to that god
who greeted me at his gates with his throat full of trumpets
and his tears full of shame
as his trembling palms collected the cinders
of his children's crime.

I know what holy is.
I know the soul is shaped like a bowl.
I know the lies we try to fill it with
and the orchards inside
we too often spill.

But my lover's shoes were laced with guitar strings
and when I walked beside
there was a silo in my chest.
There was a field full of sun.
There was a river full of gold that we left
to pick our sweet hearts from the trees
that kept uprooting tombstones
so the names of the dead would crumble into poems.

Write me down like this:
Say my ashes never made the news.
Say the jury was full of shotguns.
Then say the snow that is falling on the tip of your tongue
will refuse to melt away.
Say this to the kids hiding their heartbeats
from their father's fists.

I planted the garden of my kiss.
I opened the night with my teeth.
I loved so hard that when you press your ear to the track

the train they hear coming will still be my chest,
a rumbling harpoon,
a sky they can bury.

Look at that moon.
I am a pebble in her hand,
a harmonica held to the mouth of the river
where nothing ever

burns.

THE JEWELRY STORE

At the jewelry store
where the shiny pieces of glass
rest in rings of metal
that shine just like the nickels I spend
on Pop Rocks at Chick's candy store

the woman behind the counter
with the burlap skin
and the windproof hair
looks up from her nail file
and tells my mother
I am one "adorable little boy."

Immediately
I brace for impact,
for the car ride home
and the litany of things we will do
to fix me.

That night after dinner
I dig to the bottom of my fire-red toy box
'til I find the doll with the golden hair.
I cradle her in my arms
and I wait for my mother to see me.

When she does
she smiles so big
I decide love
is a silent auction
and I am worth more sold.

They wanna make us something.
They wanna toothpick our bones
and keep us between their teeth.

My teeth used to be so crooked
they were the only things the kids made fun of me
more than the crooked way I dressed, walked, talked.

Listen,
I am tired of wearing braces,
from my burning temples to my cold feet
from the slack in my rope
to the machine in my heartbeat.

Every closet is a Russian doll
with another inside.

By the time my mother finally found the nerve
to call me her gay daughter
I was searching for the nerve to describe
the son in my eyes
the shadow of the boy I might be
or the boy I might still love.

For the official gay record
I never left him.
He left me because of the mirror I was.
Because of the pretty he had to hold on his arm
to find a home in his own skin.

In New York City
I search for the home in my own skin
when a woman grabs me by the neck of my coat
and drags me from the ladies' room
like dog on a chain

and I am torn
between confused gratitude
and the urge to bark my pretty name
into her face 'til she can taste the smoke
of my father's pink cigar.

LADY,

do you have any idea
how many scars I already have
in the shape of this *boxing* match?

I do not wear a welcome mat
on my chest
just so people can walk all over it
fumbling with the keys
to the locks they keep building
for the doors I keep opening
hoping someone will see the rainforest growing
in my living room.

See how many ecosystems
can exist in one redwood tree.

Maybe
what you think is a tough fist
is really a tired ballerina
curling her arms around her knees.

Either way,
I can guarantee a haircut
will never tell you anything about someone's gender,
who they love, or how they fuck.

But I'll keep growing out my short temper
for the next time I have the *opportunity*
to tell someone in my queer community:

Look,
I'm about as butch
as a Swedish male figure skater.

As for dyke, I will happily dance
in that music box for tonight,

but tomorrow
when I pull the word *faggot*
from the shotgun of a frat boy's throat,
then send it in a love letter to my love
so she can scratch it down my back,

please believe
I am taking back
every Bible Belt that has ever cracked against our spines,
every night I drove through Kansas
with, I swear to god, a pink barrette in my pocket
in case I had to split-second decide
if WOMAN would be a safer armor than THIS

when his flashing blue lights
gave me ten seconds to pick
what target he'd be more likely to miss.

Officer,
I'd be willing to bet your arrows
would look a whole lot sharper in my cupid hands
than in the dull hatchet of your hate,
than in the way you spit the word *ma'am* down my throat
like I might swallow it in the same gulp as my pride
when you decide who I am.

Remember pride is *my* parade,
built from the fairy wings of boys
who bulldozed your barricades.

The day you claimed AIDS was "a gift of god"
our wheels started spinning
like Christ turning over in his grave
for every gender-bent, holy-knuckled trans kid
who's taken a knife blade to the gut,
every bloodhound who's ever gnawed on her pronoun
like her self-given name
was not a stained glass cathedral
their boots could only pray to find soul enough to touch.

Now ask me what I am.
I'll tell you all of the above
and none of what they've ever listed.

I will say I have never cared to *Be*
nearly as much as I care to *Become*.

We are all instruments
pulling the bows across our own lungs,
windmills still startling in every storm.

Have you ever seen a newborn blinking at the light?
I want to do that every day.
I want to know what the kite called itself
when it got away,

when it escaped into the night,
that jewelry case of sparkling star,
where the face of the moon is always winking
at some adorable boy
with a pink cigar.

ANDREW

When I was a kid I would secretly
call myself Andrew.
I would tug at the crotch of my pants
the way only pubescent boys do.
Ran around pounding on my bare chest like Tarzan.
It's not that I thought I'd grow up to be a man.
I just never thought I'd grow up to be a woman either.

From what I could tell neither
of those categories fit me.

But believe me
I knew from a very young age to
never say, "Dad, this Adam or Eve thing
isn't really working for me. What about
all the people in-between?"

In the third grade
Lynette Lyons asked me where all of my Barbies were.
I lied and told her I got in trouble
and my mother took them away.
I didn't dare say, "Barbie sucks, Lynette."

And for the record: so does G.I Joe.

I want to grow into something
nobody has ever seen before
and gender is just one of the ways
we are boxed in and labeled
before we are able to speak
who we believe we are
or who we dream we will become.

Like drumbeats forever changing their rhythm
I am living today as someone
I had not yet become yesterday,
and tonight I will borrow only pieces
of who I am right now
to carry with me to tomorrow.

No, I'm not gay.
No, I'm not straight.
And I'm sure as hell not bi-sexual, damnit.
I am whatever I am when I am it.

Loving whoever you are when the stars shine
and whoever you'll be when the sun rises,
crew cuts or curls
or that really bad hair phase in-between.

I like steam
rising from the body of a one-night stand.
I like holding hands
for three months before kissing.

I like imagining your body is Saturn,
my body ten thousand rings wrapped around you.

You wanted to be a Buddhist nun once.
Last night you held my cervix between your fingers.
I thanked gods I don't even believe in for you changing.

Tell me we'll be naming our children Beautiful
and nothing else.

Tell Barbie she can go now.
Tell G.I Joe to put his gun down and find a boyfriend.
Or a girlfriend.   Or a girl-boyfriend.
Fuck it, G.I Joe just needs a friend.
He's plastic, and not even the kind of plastic that bends.

I want to bend in a thousand directions like the sun does.
Like love does.
Like time might stop
so the hands of the clock can hold each other.

We can hold each other
like I held these words for too many years
on the tip of my tongue…

"I am my mother's daughter.
I am midnight's sun.
You can find me on the moon
waxing and waning,
my heart full of petals,
every single one begging love me, love me
love me.

Whoever I am.
Whoever I become."

"Activist"

In the middle
of the Pacific Ocean
there is a mass
twice the size of Texas
formed entirely
from the trash of plastic.

There is a four-hundred-pound sea turtle
about to swallow
what she thinks
is a jellyfish.

We say jellyfish
have no hearts.

We say we do.

Jesus said, "Forgive them Father
for they do not know what they are doing."

Is that true?
Do we not know what we have done?

Over five million people
have died in wars in the Congo
fighting for the minerals
that make our cell phones.

A tactic of this war
is to rape the women,
then cut off their lips and arms,

and AT&T can still convince me

to reach out

and gut someone.

Gospel Salt

Sometimes I get so nervous when I speak
I can feel my heartbeat in my tongue.
And my heartbeat talks faster than an auctioneer
but this is the last place
I would ever try to sell you something from.

When I get really scared
I imagine my enormous grandmother
is standing behind me
with her pipe-organ arms
hugged tight around my chest.

She says, "Listen, I know you run your mouth
so your mind can rest."

Now rest

is no broken levy staring up at the water.
It is the bite marks a mother leaves on the hurricane
while her daughter climbs to the 9th ward rooftop
to spray paint, "We are still here."

Yes we are.

While some days we will barely get our feet wet
most of the time we'll have to wake
and shake the tidal wave off our music stands
to make space for the notes
of a brass-knuckled saxophone
carrying the tattered hope
of the ocean's prayer.

All these words
are just paper boats praying they can get there.

Tell me we will get there
before we come up broke,
believing that people, like levies,
have to hold themselves together
when often it's the falling apart

that gives them the grace
that ensures no one ever
builds a condo over their open hearts.

Three years after Katrina
I found a sea shell
beneath an oak tree in New Orleans City Park.
I can still hold it to my ear
and hear the song the folk singer sang
the night she left so much blood on her guitar strings
and I knew I had never before been touched right,

knew we could be instruments
if we could just let our kite strings
be tuned by the lightning.

Tune me to the thunder.
I am already shaking like a matador's hands,
like California shook in the 1906 earthquake
when 28,000 buildings fell
and the people said, "When 28,000 buildings fall
do you know how many walls are no longer there?"

All that was left between them
was the gospel salt of their sweat
as they carried each other from the rubble to the street
where each night they carried the piano
to be played by a new refugee.

Some wishes can only be made on the stars' dust.

I know most of the time my shine
cannot hold a match to my rust.
So ask me about the rain.
I'll tell you my mother says, "The thing
about wheelchairs is they keep you looking up."
Says, "Forests may be gorgeous
but there's nothing more alive than a tree
that learns how to grow in a cemetery."

So when my grandmother died
I started wearing her thimbles on my fingers
when I'd type out poems,
hoping every key I'd type
would sound like a footstep of someone coming home,
the way my friend came home from Iraq
and named his baby daughter Viva.

We have all fought for our lives
more than we know,
survived our own questions.

How does one grieve a poisoned sea, a bleeding gulf?
Can even the moon handle that kind of gravity,
that pull to surrender?

I say science can split an atom.
But what if Eve could put Adam back together
by reminding him the garden is just a seed
sometimes so small it can fit on the tip of your tongue?

Say, "flint."
Say, "spark."

Say this is me hitchhiking with a green thumb,
hoping to grow something in the trust
of someone picking me up
on a day I have fallen for the wreckage.

Remind me
that the most fertile lands were built by the fires of volcanoes.
Plant my feet in the one thing that flowers

when everything else erupts. Usman,
an immigrant from Pakistan,
could not stop saying, "Brother, Brother, Brother,"
to the Jewish man whose hand he held
down ninety-eight flights of stairs
to escape the fall of the Twin Towers.

That is the only hour I can set my heart to.
The moment we realize sometimes
it is the metal in the wind chimes that reminds us
how soft the breeze is.

And maybe my grandmother only believed in Jesus
because she believed He came back
wearing that whip on His back like a halo.

Either way, this world
has picked me enough times for the madness vase
for me to know sanity is not
running from the window
when the lightning comes.

It's turning the thunder into grace,
knowing sometimes the break in your heart
is like the hole in the flute.

Sometimes it's the place
where the music come through.

CLOSE FOR COMFORT

We were the distance.
We were the too close for comfort.
We were the never comfortable.

We were the one hour a week
our therapists looked forward
to going to work.

That's definitely not true.
We couldn't afford therapy.

We were the lie through your teeth
getting caught in our own bite.

We were the junkyard dog
with someone's heart in his jaw
saying, "Listen, I'm just really scared
to be alone at night."

We were the meteor thinking twice.

We were the millionaire's lawn boy
fucking a debutant in the shed.
When they told us we were terrible in bed,
we said, "We're awesome on a tractor."

We were the ones who looked like slackers
but we were not the slackers.

We were bringing harmonicas to yoga class
saying, "If I'm gonna breathe this world deep
I'm gonna get a song out of it."

We were burning every McDonald's billboard
that said, "Loving it."
Every time we read a poem we were killing it.

We were trigger happy to trigger each other.
Whenever someone left we'd say,
"My father punches like those footsteps."

But we were the spike in the punch,
the bar fight at the AA meeting.

When I started saying, "My sober hurts,"
you started screaming, "Let's become quicksand in reverse!"

And we were Banksy on an overpass in New Orleans
spray-painting porch lights on the hurricane.

We were welcome mats for the un-forgiven.
We never sold our windpipes to make a living.

We were the letters sent to the wrong address,
but opened anyway.

We opened anyway.

We were the bearded women.
We were the genderqueers with Saran Wrap binders.
My mother said, "You've left me with nothing

to wrap the casserole with."

But we were learning to hear "I love you"
in everything our mothers said

because we were the see-through.
We were the glass doors everyone kept running into,
trying to learn how to shatter
without hurting someone.

We were the gay boy scouts
telling their fathers they're gonna quit.
We were the closet with nothing in it.

We brought our umbilical chords to show and tell.
You stopped trying to make friends
by giving away the sweets in your lunchbox.

We started holding stethoscopes
to our enemies' heartbeats.
We started listening

while we were bleeding
on the hotel bed sheets.
We were the crime scenes
our lovers swallowed chalk for.
Sometimes we were the wars we didn't believe in.

But we were saying, "Bin Laden should have had a trial."
We were saying, "Bush should have had a trial."

We were conviction.

We were a black woman saying, "Andrea Gibson,
do you have any idea how much privilege it takes to
think it's cool to dress poor?"

We were the day the white kids learned why
they were not the ones getting followed
around the store.

We were the heartbreak of truth.
We were the willing to break even more.

We were the Fahrenheit
of a monkey wrench in a heart valve.
We were the plasma that paid the rent.

We were the word "cuddle" carved
into the wall of prison cell.

We were the "I've got your back"
kiss and tell photograph
on a coffee table in house
full of crushed glass
from every ship in a bottle
we couldn't stand
not to break out.

STAIRCASE

Across the water
a train moves slow against the trees
like the bow of an aching violin.

At my side a child
is begging her mother for milk.
The mother is a broken staircase with fresh paint.
Someday the daughter's dreams will fall through
and I will turn my chest into an elevator
right before she tells me
she's claustrophobic.

For now I say, *"Listen to that train.*
It is full of milk."

The mother grabs the daughter by the sleeve,
pulls her down the beach.
On the shore the daughter finds a pebble
the color of a wedding gown,
puts it in her mouth,
crookeds her teeth,
is no longer hungry.

I dream I am a prince
or a knight
in shining removable armor.

My love's last lover is a sword
I keep falling on.
I think too much when I kiss.

If love did not exist
I would be so goddamn sane
my poems would be billboards.
Suburbia would be enough.
I would not have to gut myself
to find my spine
crushed into powder
and brushed on her cheekbones.

My hair would not be a hummingbird's nest.
My mind would not have to move so fast to rest.

I would not be in North Carolina
tearing flowers from the motel flowerpots,
searching for a love-me-not I can drop like a guillotine
on my own gallop chest.

It is incredible what kind of mess I can make
with a nine-hour drive and an unanswered text.

Yes, that is me
crying to the tollbooth man.

I say,
"In the ghost town of our love
there is a player piano
trying to prove it can make music
without being touched.
My fingertips miss her so much."

He hands me no change.
Tells me there's a Laundromat down the highway
that is also a bar.
I could make a clean getaway.
I could fall off the wagon and catch
a freight train of insanity straight through this mountain.

I could at the very least wash my clothes
so I could for once in my life know
what it's like to have control of the spin cycle,

what's it's like to know
what the yarn knows of sweaters,
how to hold myself together.

Love, I know it is not sexy to make-out
with someone who so constantly
has their foot in their mouth.
But remember
I am also the one who told you
I want to feel you like the lifelines on the palms of Jesus
felt the nails go through.

I want to make popcorn with you, with the lid off.
Yes, that's sexy talk.

Yes, I'm freaky.
Yes, I heard the bartender say
it is not holy water if it doesn't burn going down

and you are hot
enough to keep me sober
on a Saturday night on Bourbon Street.

I told her,
"You have a heart of gold
and I am kneeling in your bloodstream
panning for the only thing that has ever felt like home."

Across the water a train moves
slow against the trees, and I say, "Listen
to that train. Let's follow it
wherever it goes."

TRAFFIC

In Texas
when the cop pulls you over
for driving in the HOV lane,
because, *he* claims,
"There is no passenger in the passenger seat,"

say, "God is my copilot. I REFUSE
to be punished for your heathen inability
so see the Lord *everywhere*!"

Just kidding.
Don't say that.

LEPRECHAUN

My penis
was an awkward leprechaun
that had not gotten lucky
nearly as much as it had gotten bored
standing patiently in my pants
while the rest of me
read self-help books
on how to look sexy in green

until the day
I met your mouth,
a St. Patrick's Day parade,
your tongue, a float
you kept throwing candy from.

You made me so hot
the first time you touched me
I burned down a Christmas tree,

put the star on top of the four-leaf clover
I had built from two three-leaf clovers
and some crazy glue.

I am crazy about you,
and not because of your personality.
Everybody has a personality.

You have a tarp
and an ass
that makes me want to objectify
you in my feminist theory class.

And yes, professor, I do
think that statement deserves an A+
if only for the way it fucks
the confession booth,

thrusts its brothel
into the Baptist
of my youth.

At eleven–years–old
I told my mother
"There is something wrong with my body.
My underwear are constantly full of pee."

"Are you sure it's pee?" she asked.

I said, "What else could it be?"

But I knew

it was Satan
with his evil snakes
poking around my holy.
It was my jackrabbit Elvis pelvis
making friends with the living room pillows.

My mother said.
"What did you do to the pillows?
They have no fluff left."

I did not confess
I had ruffled their feathers,
I had buried my hump in their soft.

I did not say, "Mother,
if Mary was really a virgin
are you sure we can trust
she was ever touched by the hand of god?"

I tell my lover,
there is a Bible on my bookshelf
I need you to smack me with.
There is an anchor I am still pulling up
to free all the parts of myself
still floating on Noah's Ark.

Right between the zebras and the penguins
my kink side is curled up in a ball,
biting its claws,
begging the rain to stop.

You should never trust a ship
that won't let you get off.

You should never let your leprechaun
wear a cross to the parade in your pants.

But the moral of the story?
Never ever ever ever fuck the pillows
on your mother's living room couch.

Fuck the pillows in your own bedroom
'til you find someone
with feathers in her hair
and a Christmas tree burning
in her holy unholy mouth.

Marriage

"James Bond was also called "Mr. Kiss Kiss Bang Bang."

I tell her this on the flight
back from our trip to San Diego.
I tell her this while wearing my gas station sunglasses
and my spy hat.

I lean close to her ear in my sultry-sultry and say,
"From this day forward
I would like you to call me Mr. Kiss Kiss Bang Bang.
I don't care if we're at the dog park
or at the olive bar at the grocery store
or if we're on a camping trip in the wilderness
or if we're baking muffins
with my Aunt Susan on her farm in Canada.
From now on you are to call me only
Mr. Kiss Kiss Bang Bang."

She is reading a book of nerd poetry.
She doesn't look up from the page.

I want to make her my horny librarian.
I want to show her my spy moves.

"Kiss Kiss Bang Bang," I whisper.
"And don't forget the Mister."

She turns the page.

"Bang bang. Bang bang."

Nothing.

"Kiss kiss."

Nothing.

"Mr. Bang Ba—"

"No," she says. "Stop.
I'm not gonna call you that. Ever."

But I know she will.

Some night when I'm walking around our house
wearing only my ill-fitting boy panties,
my belly bloated with three bad movies worth of popcorn,
when I'm standing in our bathroom mirror
picking the kernels from my teeth,
she'll come up behind me.......
"Bang bang, bang bang."

We'll make love like fugitives.
After we'll smoke cigars while the dog watches
from his corner of the sex room.

"So you're into bondage?" I'll say.

"Yes," she'll say, patting my popcorned belly. "James Bondage."

And that,
of course,
is what marriage is.

CLASS

The hang out parking lot
was in the center of town.

In the parking lot there was a gas station,
a car wash, and a convenience store.

In the convenience store there was a fried chicken place
that doubled as a pizza shop.

In the pizza shop Peggy had one tooth left.

She was chain smoking
while making pizza in a hairnet
when that tooth fell from her mouth
and landed on a medium pepperoni.
She closed the lid to the box and said, "Kid,
you have no idea what these gums can do
to a man in bed. Trust me,
teeth just get in the way."

I had just enough bite to believe her.

It was my third summer working
in the convenience store freezer.
I wore a snowsuit in August and smelled
like a truckload of frostbit Budweiser cans.

But I knew love
at noon every Sunday
when I took the locks off of the beer case.
Even the preacher came straight from church
to call me an angel.

I listened to the bells on the door
and stole more than enough bottles for myself
to understand that everyone's chest
is a living room wall
with awkwardly placed photographs
hiding fist-shaped holes.

I was eighteen years old.
My boyfriend was a butcher at the IGA.
My body was a hotel safe I didn't trust.
My bedroom window was so close to the ocean
everyone I knew had salt in their wounds
and a rifle in their truck.

I carried most of what was shot in my tear ducts,
but where I come from you never let what you carry fall.

You carry your grandmother's laundry
to the clothesline where she will teach you,
"Always hang your underwear on the inside, hidden
between the towels and the blankets."

For eighteen years my heartbeat
like a good ol' boy
taking a baseball bat to a mailbox,

like a mill worker on the picket line;
talking about the size of the trout
his daughter caught,

like my father
smoking a Marlboro Red
while cutting the grass
after a twelve-hour day.

That is always what I think of
when I think of class:
his blue collar against his red neck.
You know where that word
comes from, right? The sun,
beating against his back.

But at eighteen that sun
was something I was desperate to outrun,
so I stared at the notches on the wall
that measured my height, praying someday
they would all lay down like tracks
I could cross to the other side.

The other side...

Tonight
I am in a coffee shop
full of people talking art
and green politics.
In a moment I will take the stage
but I won't hear my heart
over my mouth.

I won't hear anything
but Peggy punching that time clock
like someday she might actually
knock it out.

A Letter to the Playground Bully, from Andrea, Age 8 ½

Maybe there are cartwheels in your mouth.
Maybe your words will grow up to be gymnasts.
Maybe you have been kicking people with them by accident.

I know some people get a whole lot of rocking
in the rocking chair
and the ones who don't
sometimes get rocks in their voice boxes
and their voice boxes become slingshots.
Maybe you think my heart
looks like a baby squirrel.

But you absolutely miss
when you tell the class I have head lice
because I 100 percent absolutely
do not have head lice

and even if I do
it's a fact that head lice prefer clean heads over dirty ones.
So I am clean as a whistle
on a teapot.

My mother says it is totally fine
if I blow off steam
as long as I speak in an octave
my kindness can still reach.

My kindness knows mermaids
never ever miss their legs in the water
because there are better ways to move
through an ocean than kicking.

So guess what: if I ever have my own team,
I am picking everyone first,

even the worst kid
and the kid with the stutter
like a skipping record
because I know all of us are scratched,
even if you can't hear it when we speak.

My mother says a lot of people have heartbeats
that are knocking on doors that will never open,
and I know my heart is a broken freezer chest
because I can never keep anything frozen.

So no, I am not "always crying."
I am just thawing outside the lines.

And even if I am "always crying"
it is a fact that salt is the only reason
everything floats so good in the Dead Sea.

And just because no one ever passes notes to me
doesn't mean I am not super duper.
In fact, my super duper might be a buoy or a paper boat
the next time your nose is stuck up the river

because it is a fact
that our hearts stop for a milisecond every time we sneeze
and some people's houses have too much dust.

Some people's fathers are attics.
I've heard attics have monsters in their walls
and shaky stares. I think if I lived in a house with an attic
I'd nightmare a burglar in my safety chest,
and maybe I'd look for rest
in the sticks and stones

because my mother says
a kid can only swallow so much punch
before he's drunk on his own fist.

But the only drunk I have ever known
was sleeping in the alley behind my church,
and Jesus turned his water into wine,
so even god has his bad days.

But on your bad days couldn't you just say,
"I'm having a bad day,"
instead of telling me I'm stupid or poor
or telling me I dress like a boy

because maybe I am a boy *and* a girl.
Maybe my name is Andrea Andrew, so what.
It is a fact that bumblebees have hair on their eyeballs
and people, also, should comb
through everything they see.

For instance, an anchorman is not a sailor,
and the clouds might be a pillow fight.

My mother says,
"Every bird perched on a telephone wire
will listen to the conversations running through its feet
to decide the direction of its flight."

So I know every word we speak
can make hurricanes in people's weather veins
or shine their shiny shine.

So maybe sometime somebody
could sit beside me on the bus
and I could say, "Guess what, it is a fact
that manatees have vocal chords
even though they don't have ears,
and Beethoven made music
even when he could no longer hear."

And I know every belt that has hit someone's back
is still a belt that was built to hold something up.

And it is fact that Egyptians slept on pillows made of stone
but it's not hard for me to dream
that maybe one day you'll write me back
like the day I wrote the lightning bug to say,
"I smashed my mason jar and I threw away the lid."

I didn't want to take a chance that I'd grow up to be a war.

I want to be a belly dance, or an accordion, or a pogo stick
or the fingerprints the mason left
in the mortar between the bricks
to prove that he was here,
that he built a roof over someone's head
to keep the storm from their hope.

My mother says that's why we all were born.

And I think she's right.
So write back soon.

Sincerely yours.

Yellow Bird

My Uncle Billy is the leading
Little Debbie's Snack Cake salesman
in all of North America.
From Vancouver, British Columbia to Miami, Florida
nobody sells more Fudge Rounds,
Swiss Rolls or Nutty Bars than him.

My family is incredibly proud of this fact.
We tell it to strangers, to the prospective husbands of our nieces,
to the clerk at the drugstore.
We whisper it in church.
"Did you hear about Billy? Yeah, he's the leading
 Little Debbie's Snack Cake salesman in all of North America."

And I
will never write a poem
that will ever come close
to matching the grandeur of that.

"So ya won the Nobel Prize, did ya? That's nice.
Did ya hear Billy put six hundred cream pies
on the rack at the IGA and in three days
that rack was fricken empty…"

Why is art the first class to be dropped by any public school?
Why are music rooms empty in junior highs
from New York City to Nashville, Tennessee?
How can you burn CD after CD after CD
while filling your tank with an infinite amount of gas
like the war is worth funding
but music isn't?

Our culture is a prison
and the only one with a key is little Emmy Jones
covering every inch of her standardized test
with the best number-two pencil version of *Starry Night*
anyone has ever seen.

And yes,
there is a hummingbird in her chest.
Its wings are beating eighty times a second
for the second it takes you and I to see that
Dr. King did not write a speech called "I Have a Dream."
He wrote a poem called 'I Have a Dream.'

I don't know if god will ever have a purple heart
but I know we have a bow
we could pull above the strings of a combat boot
and make it sing
like the voice of a seven-year-old boy
staring down the barrels
of apartheid's loaded guns
screaming for the right to write stories
in his mother's tongue.

Point me in the direction of glory.
I will run towards a tiny hand
in the most wounded corner of Palestine,
dipping a brush into a can of yellow paint
to paint a feather on a wall
that is so tall only yellow birds can escape,
carrying the hearts of children
on their backs when they do.

And when their wings flap
they will make the sound of anthems
being replaced with sky.
I swear I could see their shadows
pass across your glowing face
the night you said you have never given birth to a child
but tear every single time you write a poem.

We are growing our future with every borrowed pen.
I pray tonight we will write a rainstorm
that will fall like the tears at Folsom Prison
the day Johnny Cash smashed his guitar over apathy's head.

The way Frida Khalo in the prison of her own body
had whole years when she could paint nothing but red.
But she painted through the bars
and the locked cell of her pores
the same way saxophones in New Orleans
played music underwater
knowing some of those notes
would rise up towards the air
carrying people and hope to shore.

I don't believe in the godliness of steeples
but I believe in the stained glass
and every key on every organ
that is desperate for light,

'cause we are desperate for life,
for the site of a captivated audience
refusing to be held captive in the thought
that they can only listen and watch.

Picasso said he'd paint with his own wet tongue
on the dusty floor of a jail cell if he had to.

We have to create.
It is the only thing louder than destruction.
It's the only chance the bars are gonna break,
our hands full of color
reaching towards the sky,
a brush stroke in the dark.

It is not too late.
That starry night
is not yet dry.

THE PURSUIT OF HAPPINESS

Tonight in the Iraq
there is a race to rape little girls
before they can be raped by US soldiers.

Tonight in Iran
there is a missile aimed at the hill
where Hafiz wove pieces of his spirit
into a blanket to keep us warm.

Tonight my skin is the color
of a hundred white flags
torn apart at the seams
and sewn into a body bag.

Tonight every flashing red light
is a heart threatening to quit.
The moon is a tourniquet
we will bleed through by morning.

Is this your pursuit of happiness?

The casket as small as a music box,
a mother lifting that song to her ear.
A mother filling her lungs with sand
and cradling her baby daughter
'til her own clavicle is fine as powder.

America, I dare you
to place your holy water beside her tears
and see where Jesus chooses to walk.

Heaven doesn't know your name,
only the sound of you rolling your barrels of blood
to its gates
thinking grace is something you can buy
with Muhammad's pulse.

Tell me again
how you intend to rescue their women.
How you will teach them how to read
in the schools you've turned to prisons.
How you will offer them doctors
in the hospitals you have burned
with their children inside.

Tell me how they will no longer
have to hide beneath burkas.
How you will wrap them in lace
'til they are all as conveniently rape-able
as women in the States.

Do you know how much desert sand
is on the floor of the women's shelter in my city?
Have you ever heard your skull crack on a kitchen sink?
Have you ever tried to blink the light back?

Do you know the man who beat her
had been ordered to fit five Afghani children
in a single body bag?

Is this your pursuit of happiness?

The orphanage you lit like a cigarette?
You cough and it sounds like screams.
You cancer the soil with our holy flag.
You dog tagged your son,
choke-chained his two years into eight,
then forgot his name
when you couldn't afford the gas
to drive to his funeral.

Do you know how his family loved you?
Their trust was an orchard.
Now tonight at their table
nothing is alive but his empty chair.

If you are a nation under God,
how is hell so close to your prayers?
Can you not see what you are pressing
between your palms? Bones
cannot break   into song.

A mother can never find the right place
to store an empty cradle.
A mouth can never find the right shape
to hold the lullabies it will never sing.

Tonight, if you ripped the pipelines from your throat,
if you hung them like wind chimes from the battered sky
would you remember how freedom rings?

Would you remember every river
is a lantern running without oil
and your children sing your anthem so proud,
America the Beautiful, remember?

If you stood so close to the fire
the flames caught the lashes,
if you could memorize one face fading into smoke
and never ever forget
would you let one more soldier
write his blood type on his boots?

Would you let your pursuit of happiness
steal so much god from the heart
that I know is still beating
beneath your bloody hand?

You

If you
were here
I could drive
in the HOV lane.

Loneliness
moves so

slow.

JELLYFISH
Inspired by Shira Erlichman

When the astronaut told me she needed more space
I dropped my pants to the floor
in the grocery store
hoping I could moon her into staying.

Most of us will do anything
to try and prove we are enough,
to prove our sky is not Hollywood,
our stars are not actors,
to prove the twinkle in our eye
isn't an infection.

I can look in almost any direction
and say, "That's the way to go."
But I've learned this is how to stay:
skipping moon rocks across my own puddle dive
even when I've been clipped from the mother ship
so I can still say, "I bet you smell like butterfly.
But I bet you dream cocoon."

My heart is a runway.
I've been staring at the sky since my love took off.
Will you be my friend?
Will you poem me a porch swing?
Will you punch me in the tough, just once?

I'm ready to reset my bones,
ready to swing-set my ribcage
so the next time somebody pushes me away
I'll swing right back to that chisel
with my marble spine.
Go ahead, build me.
Go ahead, throw me at the storm
like a fisherman's prayer.

Do you ever think about god's ears?
Wonder if the levy broke a promise?
Wonder if the wrecking ball
was trying to run its fingers soft across the bricks
but its head was just too heavy?

Before you become my friend,
picnic with my rubble,
road trip with everyone I left in the dust,
do the laundry from the last time I was loaded,
found my trigger
and we woke with the sheet pulled above our heads
praying the mortician could make us pretty.

None of us are pretty.
But our ugly has an alibi.
And our gorgeous has a sand collection,
a baby sister, and two harmonicas
we keep blowing off
for that flute we carved from our wrist.

Put your lips there.
Tell me there is music in my blood.
Then tell me there is more in my light.
Hang me chandelier from the last night
I believed this life had to hurt so much.

I am done kneeling in the church
of steepled smokestacks.
Done star gazing my own train crash.
Give me wind sprints.
Tell me my fingerprints are the shape of ripples
on a frozen lake.

Tell me my coal mind
will never collapse on my heart.

I'll tell you these poems are my birthmarks,
and I came so close to having them removed
I even kept a voice box cutter hidden in my shoe
the day her flight took off.

But the runway—it's made of marble, made of gush,
made of windmill, made of salt,
and there is a sea of hope chests
in every word I speak
praying to be opened by the night
with its belly full of yield.

Pull the shield from my wingspan.
Teach me why the candle wax says *thank you* to the flame.
Tell me how your mother says your name
like an orchard going bloom.

A doctor once told me I feel too much.
I said, "So does God.
That's why you can see the Grand Canyon from the moon."

We are a telescope of riverbed.
We are empty lockets melting into gold.
We are hearts breaking   bread.

Fold me in the napkin poem.
Pull the tinsel from my hair
from all the past I could not let go.
My gills are adjusting to the air,
the story husk peeling from my bones.

My bones
know the song of our tears
dripping from the faucet,
ticking like a metronome.

I know there is better music.
Even in this cabin full of fever.
Tonight I'm catching nothing but the lightning bug.
My body is a mason jar,
transparent as a jellyfish.

I wish for a heart you can see straight through,
for a voice that glows in the dark,
and a few really good friends
to say, "That's the way to go."

CONTACT SOLUTION

In Los Angeles I slept for three nights
on the floor of a tiny room
full of tools to make jewelry.
Every morning I'd slip my fingers
into the silver rings on the walls
and say "yes" to something
I could not yet name.

In San Francisco
my friend lifted me off my feet
and hugged me like a chiropractic appointment.
That night on stage I could hear my bones
crackling like a campfire.

We headed for the redwoods.
Holy heaven, I am so short.

I found a tree house that day
I would have given anything
to have a sleepover in.

In Idaho I spent the night in a field
full of cottonwood and bumblebees.
That day I could taste the honey
more than the sting
and I fell asleep early to the songs of crickets
and a river named after the bees.

In Portland a stranger busted me out of jail.
I buried at least three of my prisons that day,
the radio dial pulling the sun through the gray.

In Seattle I watched a plane land on water
for the first time in my whole life.
Amazing, how light you do not have to be
to float.

Crossing the Canadian border to Vancouver
I was sure I was unknowingly
transporting illegal drugs or heavy artillery.
(Worrying keeps me in touch with my family.)

Last night on the flight back to Colorado
I wrote her name on a tiny piece of paper
and tucked it inside the Sky Mall Magazine
on the page that sells fancy pillows
that mold to the shape of your head.

Today I slept too late, watered the garden,
and wondered if our dog has forgotten my face.

If tomorrow morning
I can open the medicine cabinet
and throw away her bottle of contact solution
I will thank the road
for finally bringing me home.

The Vinegar Club

I threw tantrums.
You threw bottle caps from the top of the Ferris wheel.
When the creek said, "Laugh until your sides split,"
we didn't wonder if we'd grow up to be happy.

We buried time capsules in the dirt beside my house
and dug them up a day later.
So much time had passed.

We'd been cowboys, bank robbers, and the Jackson Five.
Jeffrey Bartlett had kissed a girl on the mouth
and said he saw fireworks
just like the movies said we all would.

Some things come true.
God, for example.

The day you peed your pants
in the middle of the spelling bee
I was sitting beside you
chewing on my pony tail
with the angst of a trucker stuck in a bunny suit.

When the puddle hit the floor
I pulled the ponytail from my teeth
and started crying for the both of us.

On the playground
I wanted to tell you your Hula-Hoop
could be the Jolly Green Giant's halo.
But you were wearing pants from the lost and found box
so I said, "You Hula-Hoop like Elvis. He's a king, ya know."

That year we found four dead puppies
in a plastic bag beneath the crab apple tree.
I knew immediately that puppies are expensive to raise.
Children are, too.

There were months when the radiator of your ribcage
wouldn't keep your heart warm
even though your father kept pounding on it
with the back end of a broomstick.

You could go the entire week
without speaking a word.

I knew the silence kept your spine
from becoming their wishbone.
So for you, I let my hair down
to cover my eyes
as the rescue scenes in your movie
kept escaping us
and I laughed at my own jokes
'til you told me they weren't funny.

But I was funny to look at.

I wore folded pieces of tinfoil around my crooked teeth,
stuffed plastic Smurfs in my underwear
to build a penis that wasn't there,
and was constantly pretending to swear.

"Holy ship!" I'd say.
"Can you believe that mother sucker?" I'd say,
pointing at Tommy McCray's newborn brother
breastfeeding in his mother's lap.

You could never understand ship like that,
public nudity on the little league bleachers
when so many folks were trying to hide
closets in their skeletons
so their funny bones could out-dress that man in the moon
on the nights he wore light like a costume,
like that plastic sheriff's badge
you couldn't stop staring at
on the floor of your bedroom.

But god be my witness when I say
you were humming miracles
into your harmonica wrist
that day we climbed that rusted fence
and pressed our hands in the wet cement
to prove we were permanent
like the dye in our mother's hair,
meaning: we are definitely here,
but we can grow out.

We can run away with the carnival
and build a Tilt-a-Whirl with our own grace.

Ya know, your face
never looked so fun-house mirror
as it did the day you finally found a way to escape.

You terrible speller.
You busted compass.

My heart is still a letter jacket
I am waiting to give to someone sweet.
I still stuff things in my underwear
but I never *pretend* to swear.

We don't know shit
about walking a mile in somebody else's shoes
'til we know almost everything
about our own bare feet.

And my feet have always been about as cold
as the creek can get
but when fear reaches the ocean it turns to salt

and maybe it's nobody's fault that god
only held so many shells to his ear.

So I slap my heart against the dock
and grab my own windpipe
to beat the truth from my throat.
I tear the wallpaper from my skin
and I search the oak for its knots.
I throw these rocks at my tantrums, and I listen
for where the windows are.

Can you hear that, friend?
Can you hear the breaking?
It is the holiest part.

I Sing the Body Electric, Especially When My Power's Out

I have weather veins.
They are especially sensitive
to dust storms and hurricanes.

When I'm nervous my teeth chatter
like a wheelbarrow collecting rain.
I am rusty when I talk.
It's the storm in me.

The doctors say someday
I might not be able to walk.
It's in my blood like the iron.
My mother is tough as nails.
She held herself together

the day she could no longer hold my niece.
We said, "Our kneecaps are our prayer beds.
Everyone can walk farther on their kneecaps
than they can on their feet."

This is my heartbeat.
Like yours, it is a hatchet.
It can build a house
or tear one down.

My mouth is a fire escape.
The words coming out
don't care that they are naked.
There is something burning in here.

When it burns I hold my own shell to my ear,
listen for the parade from when I was seven,

when the man who played the bagpipes
wore a skirt.
He was from Scotland.
I wanted to move there.

Wanted my spine to be the spine
of an unpublished book,
my faith the first and last page.

The day my ribcage became monkey bars
for a girl hanging on my every word
they said, "You are not allowed to love her."
Tried to take me by the throat
to teach me, "You are not a boy."

I had to unlearn their prison speak,
refusing to make wishes on the star
on the sheriff's chest.

I started talking to the stars in the sky instead.
I said, "Tell me about the big bang."
The stars said, "It hurts to become."

I carry that hurt on the tip of my tongue
and whisper, "bless your heart"
every chance I get
so my family tree can be sure
I have not left.

You do not have to leave to arrive.

I am learning this slowly.
So sometimes when I look in the mirror
my eyes still look like the holes
in the shoes of the shoe-shine man,

my hands are busy on the wrong things.
Some days I call my arms "wings"
while my head is in the clouds.
It will take me a few more years to learn flying
is not pushing away the ground.

But safety isn't always safe.
You can find one on every gun.

I am aiming to do better.

This is my body.
My exhaustion pipe
will never pass inspection,
and still my lungs know how to breathe
like a burning map
every time I get lost
in the curtain of her hair.

Find me by the window
following my past
to a trail of blood in the snow.

The night I opened my veins
the doctor who stitched me up
asked me if I did it for attention.

For the record,
if you have ever done anything for attention,
this poem is attention.
Title it with your name.

It will pace the city bridge
every midnight you stand
kicking at your shadow,
staring at the river.

It does not want to find your body
doing anything but loving what it loves.

Love what you love.
Say, "This is my body.
It is no one's but mine."

This is my nervous system,
my wanting blood,
my half-tamed addictions,
my tongue tied up
like a ball of Christmas lights.

If you put a star on the top of my tree
make sure it's a star that fell.
Make sure it hit bottom
like a tambourine,

because all of these words are just stories
for the staircase
to the top of lungs
where I sing what hurts
and the echo comes back
saying, "Bless your heart.
Bless your body.
Bless your holy kneecaps...
they are so smart.

You are so full of rain.
There is so much that's growing.
Hallelujah to your weather veins.
Hallelujah to the ache.
Hallelujah to the full and to the fall,
to the pull and to the pain.

Hallelujah to the grace
in the body,
in every cell of us all."

HOW IT ENDS

It has been four years, seven months, and six days
since the first time I saw you naked.
Since the night you ripped off your shirt,
stuck your boobs in my face and said, "Touch them."

I touched them like a diabetic third grader
opening a Snickers Bar.

You said, "Hard."
I thought, "Yes, I am."
But you are so soft.
I said, "Your lips are like whale blubber."
That wasn't my best line.
But it worked.

Today in the grocery store
I found one of your hairs in my underwear.
I pulled it out in the frozen food section
and screamed, "That is so gorgeous it could kill a man!"
Good thing I'm a leprechaun.
Lucky, lucky, lucky.

Baby, I have no idea how this will end.
Maybe the equator will fall like a Hula-Hoop
from the earth's hips
and our mouths will freeze mid-kiss
on our eightieth anniversary.

Or maybe tomorrow my absolute insanity
combined with the absolute obstacle course
of your communication skills
will leave us like a love letter in a landfill.

But whatever, whenever, however this ends
I want you to know right now,
I love you forever.

I love you for the hardest mile we walked together.
For the night I collected every sharp knife in the house
and threw them one by one on the roof,
then told the sun, "Listen, show off.
For now on you are to only
give me blades of grass,
things that are growing and soft,

'cause there's this girl who says she wants
to float on her back through my bloodstream,
and when she does
I want my rivers to reach the sea."

Do you hear me, love?
Do you know the night
you told me you have a crush on my ears
I swore to never become Van Gogh?

And look! They're both still there!

Just like my firefly heart
is still right there in your glass jar.
I've never trusted anybody more
to poke enough holes in the lid.

So on the nights you sleep like a ballerina
I try to snore like a piccolo,
and I press my lips to your holy temples
and whisper, "I crash into things in the dark.
Even when the lights are on.
And I am wrong more often than I am writing,
and even then, I am often wrong."

But when my friends
are in the bathroom at the bar
rolling dollar bills into telescopes
and claiming they can see god,
I will come to you holding my grandmother's Bible.
I will press it to your chest,
and I will bless it with your breath.

And when you ask if I want to role play
alter boys fucking in the church kitchen
during Sunday mass

I will say, "Hell yes!

But only if you leave a hickey on my ass
in the shape of Jesus' palm.
So I can be sure I got nailed.

Love,
you will never lose me to the wind.
You are the lightning
that made me fill my chest with candles.
You are the thunder clapping
for the poem nobody else wants to hear.

You are an icicle's tear
watering a tulip on the first day of spring.
You melt me alive.
You kiss me deep as my roots will reach,
and I want nothing more than to be an eyelash
fallen on your cheek,

a thing collected by your fingers
and held like a wish.

I promise, whatever I do
I will always try my best to come true.

Notes and Credits

"Maybe I Need You"— inspired by the song "Baby I Need You", by Kim Taylor

"Ashes" — written in collaboration with the music of Chris Pureka

"The Jewelry Store" — inspired by the work of Kate Bornstein

"How It Ends" — inspired by the song "How It Ends", by Devotchka. Also, the line, "The night we heated our home from the steam off of our own bodies," is credited to Heather Mann.

"Yellowbird" — The line, "I have never given birth to a child, but I tear every single time I write a poem," is credited to J/J hastain

"Class" — with thanks to the work of Tara Hardy

"Gospel Salt" — Inspired by the book *A Paradise Built In Hell*, by Rebecca Solnit

About the Author

Rousing audiences internationally with her poignant message and her genuine interest in generating change, Andrea Gibson is a queer poet/activist whose work deconstructs the foundations of the current political machine, highlighting issues such as patriarchy, gender norms, white-supremacy and capitalist culture. Cementing her niche in the upper echelon of the national performance poetry slam scene, Andrea has placed in the top four on five international finals stages and was the first ever Women of the World Slam Champion in 2008. As a touring artist, Andrea has headlined everywhere from the Nuyorican Poet's Café, to Pride Fests and Lady Fests, to high schools and universities throughout the U.S. and Europe. She has been showcased on Free Speech TV, the BBC, the documentary "Slam Planet" and Independent Radio Stations worldwide. She currently a member of Vox Feminista, a multi-passionate performance tribe of radical, political performers bent on social change through cultural revolution. Andrea is an independent artist who has selfreleased five CD's, *Bullets and Windchimes, Swarm, When the Bough Breaks, "Yellowbird"* and *"Flower Boy"*. Her first book, *Pole Dancing to Gospel Hymns*, is available from Write Bloody Publishing.

New Write Bloody Books for 2011

Dear Future Boyfriend
Cristin O'Keefe Aptowicz's debut collection of poetry tackles
love and heartbreak with no-nonsense honesty and wit.

38 Bar Blues
C. R. Avery's second book, loaded with bar-stool musicality and brass-knuckle poetry.

Workin' Mime to Five
Dick Richard is a fired cruise ship pantomimist. You too can learn
his secret, creative pantomime moves. Humor by Derrick Brown.

Reasons to Leave the Slaughter
Ben Clark's book of poetry revels in youthful discovery from the heartland
and the balance between beauty and brutality.

Birthday Girl with Possum
Brendan Constantine's second book of poetry examines the invisible lines
between wonder & disappointment, ecstasy & crime, savagery & innocence.

Yesterday Won't Goodbye
Boston gutter punk Brian Ellis releases his second book of poetry,
filled with unbridled energy and vitality.

Write About an Empty Birdcage
Debut collection of poetry from Elaina M. Ellis that flirts with loss,
reveres appetite, and unzips identity.

These Are the Breaks
Essays from one of hip-hops deftest public intellectuals, Idris Goodwin

Bring Down the Chandeliers
Tara Hardy, a working-class queer survivor of incest, turns sex,
trauma and forgiveness inside out in this collection of new poems.

1,000 Black Umbrellas
The first internationally released collection of poetry
by old school author Daniel McGinn.

The Feather Room
Anis Mojgani's second collection of poetry explores storytelling and
poetic form while traveling farther down the path of magic realism.

Love in a Time of Robot Apocalypse
Latino-American poet David Perez releases his first book
of incisive, arresting, and end-of-the-world-as-we-know-it poetry.

The New Clean
Jon Sands' poetry redefines what it means to laugh, cry, mop it up and start again.

Sunset at the Temple of Olives
Paul Suntup's unforgettable voice merges subversive surrealism
and vivid grief in this debut collection of poetry.

Gentleman Practice
Righteous Babe Records artist and 3-time International Poetry Champ
Buddy Wakefield spins a nonfiction tale of a relay race to the light.

How to Seduce a White Boy in Ten Easy Steps
Debut collection for feminist, biracial poet Laura Yes Yes
dazzles with its explorations into the politics and metaphysics of identity.

Hot Teen Slut
Cristin O'Keefe Aptowicz's second book recounts stories of
a virgin poet who spent a year writing for the porn business.

Working Class Represent
A young poet humorously balances an office job with the life
of a touring performance poet in Cristin O'Keefe Aptowicz's third book of poetry

Oh, Terrible Youth
Cristin O'Keefe Aptowicz's plump collection commiserates and celebrates
all the wonder, terror, banality and comedy that is the long journey to adulthood.

OTHER WRITE BLOODY BOOKS (2003 - 2010)

Great Balls of Flowers (2009)
Steve Abee's poetry is accessible, insightful, hilarious, compelling,
upsetting, and inspiring. TNB Book of the Year.

Everything Is Everything (2010)
The latest collection from poet Cristin O'Keefe Aptowicz,
filled with crack squirrels, fat presidents, and el Chupacabra.

Catacomb Confetti (2010)
Inspired by nameless Parisian skulls in the catacombs of France,
Catacomb Confetti assures Joshua Boyd's poetic immortality.

Born in the Year of the Butterfly Knife (2004)
The Derrick Brown poetry collection that birthed Write Bloody Publishing.
Sincere, twisted, and violently romantic.

I Love You Is Back (2006)
A poetry collection by Derrick Brown.
"One moment tender, funny, or romantic, the next, visceral, ironic,
and revelatory—Here is the full chaos of life." (Janet Fitch, *White Oleander*)

Scandalabra (2009)
Former paratrooper Derrick Brown releases a stunning collection of poems written
at sea and in Nashville, TN. About.com's book of the year for poetry

Don't Smell the Floss (2009)
Award-winning writer Matty Byloos' first book of bizarre, absurd, and deliciously
perverse short stories puts your drunk uncle to shame.

The Bones Below (2010)
National Slam Champion Sierra DeMulder performs and teaches
with the release of her first book of hard-hitting, haunting poetry.

The Constant Velocity of Trains (2008)
The brain's left and right hemispheres collide in Lea Deschenes' Pushcart-Nominated
book of poetry about physics, relationships, and life's balancing acts.

Heavy Lead Birdsong (2008)
Award-winning academic poet Ryler Dustin releases his most
definitive collection of surreal love poetry.

Uncontrolled Experiments in Freedom (2008)
Boston underground art scene fixture Brian Ellis
becomes one of America's foremost narrative poetry performers.

Ceremony for the Choking Ghost (2010)
Slam legend Karen Finneyfrock's second book of poems ventures
into the humor and madness that surrounds familial loss.

Pole Dancing to Gospel Hymns (2008)
Andrea Gibson, a queer, award-winning poet who tours with Ani DiFranco,
releases a book of haunting, bold, nothing-but-the-truth ma'am poetry.

City of Insomnia (2008)
Victor D. Infante's noir-like exploration of unsentimental truth and poetic exorcism.

The Last Time as We Are (2009)
A new collection of poems from Taylor Mali, the author
of "What Teachers Make," the most forwarded poem in the world.

In Search of Midnight: the Mike Mcgee Handbook of Awesome (2009)
Slam's geek champion/class clown Mike McGee on his search for midnight
through hilarious prose, poetry, anecdotes, and how-to lists.

Over the Anvil We Stretch (2008)
2-time poetry slam champ Anis Mojgani's first collection: a Pushcart-Nominated
batch of backwood poetics, Southern myth, and rich imagery.

Animal Ballistics (2009)
Trading addiction and grief for empowerment and humor with her poetry,
Sarah Morgan does it best.

Rise of the Trust Fall (2010)
Award-winning feminist poet Mindy Nettifee
releases her second book of funny, daring, gorgeous, accessible poems.

No More Poems About the Moon (2008)
A pixilated, poetic and joyful view of a hyper-sexualized,
wholeheartedly confused, weird, and wild America with Michael Roberts.

Miles of Hallelujah (2010)
Slam poet/pop-culture enthusiast Rob "Ratpack Slim" Sturma
shows first collection of quirky, fantastic, romantic poetry.

Spiking the Sucker Punch (2009)
Nerd heartthrob, award-winning artist and performance poet,
Robbie Q. Telfer stabs your sensitive parts with his wit-dagger.

Racing Hummingbirds (2010)
Poet/performer Jeanann Verlee releases an award-winning book
of expertly crafted, startlingly honest, skin-kicking poems.

Live for a Living (2007)
Acclaimed performance poet Buddy Wakefield releases his second collection
about healing and charging into life face first.

WRITE BLOODY ANTHOLOGIES

The Elephant Engine High Dive Revival (2009)
Our largest tour anthology ever! Features unpublished work by
Buddy Wakefield, Derrick Brown, Anis Mojgani and Shira Erlichman!

The Good Things About America (2009)
American poets team up with illustrators to recognize the beauty and wonder in our
nation. Various authors. Edited by Kevin Staniec and Derrick Brown

Junkyard Ghost Revival (2008)
Tour anthology of poets, teaming up for a journey of the US in a small van.
Heart-charging, socially active verse.

The Last American Valentine:
Illustrated Poems To Seduce And Destroy (2008)
Acclaimed authors including Jack Hirschman, Beau Sia, Jeffrey McDaniel,
Michael McClure, Mindy Nettifee and more. 24 authors and 12 illustrators
team up for a collection of non-sappy love poetry. Edited by Derrick Brown

Learn Then Burn (2010)
Exciting classroom-ready anthology for introducing new writers
to the powerful world of poetry. Edited by Tim Stafford and Derrick Brown.

Learn Then Burn Teacher's Manual (2010)
Turn key classroom-safe guide Tim Stafford and Molly Meacham
to accompany *Learn Then Burn*: A modern poetry anthology for the classroom.

Knocking at the Door: Poems for Approaching the Other (2011)
An exciting compilation of diverse authors that explores the concept of the Other
from all angles. Innovative writing from emerging and established poets.

WWW.WRITEBLOODY.COM

Pull Your Books Up
By Their Bootstraps

Write Bloody Publishing distributes and promotes great books of fiction, poetry and art every year. We are an independent press dedicated to quality literature and book design, with an office in Long Beach, CA.

Our employees are authors and artists so we call ourselves a family. Our design team comes from all over America: modern painters, photographers and rock album designers create book covers we're proud to be judged by.

We publish and promote 8-12 tour-savvy authors per year. We are grass-roots, D.I.Y., bootstrap believers. Pull up a good book and join the family. Support independent authors, artists and presses.

Visit us online:

WRITEBLOODY.COM

CPSIA information can be obtained
at www.ICGtesting.com
Printed in the USA
FSHW011327060321
79231FS